RESCUE DOGS

RESCUE DOGS

Heartwarming tales of dumped dogs that have found their forever homes

Carey Edwards

Australian Working Dog Rescue

ABC
Books

Dedication

On 28 May 2013, Australian Working Dog Rescue's heart, a blue cattle dog named Chip who was the very foundation of the organisation, crossed the rainbow bridge to wait for us until we are reunited.

In recognition of Chip, and the others before him, and for those who follow after, 28 May is known to Australian Working Dog Rescue and our supporters as Tribute Day. It's a day to pay homage to the dogs who have passed; not just to working dogs, but all the dogs who have crossed the rainbow bridge and are waiting for us on the other side.

Every year on 28 May you can share your tributes to those you loved, cherished and miss on our Facebook page. A place and time dedicated to our best mates, our companions and our loved ones that aren't quite human, but nearly are.
www.facebook.com/awdri.com.au

Contents

If you pick up a starving dog and make him prosperous he will not bite you. That is the principal difference between a dog and man.

Mark Twain

Foreword

I volunteer and support many wonderful charitable organisations in Australia, but none as close to my heart as Australian Working Dog Rescue (AWDRI).

I am a passionate lover of all animals, but there will always be an extra special place in my heart for the working dog breeds. Growing up in Cairns, Far North Queensland, there were always at least two cattle dogs running amok in my backyard. Truly a part of the family, there aren't many photos of my formative life sans a puppy dog: whether it be of us playing around the backyard with Paddy or Rusty, or Mickey dog sitting in amongst the kids' circle at my seventh birthday party, playing pass the parcel. For me, there is nothing comparable to the intelligence, energy, character, devotion and loving soul of a working dog. It is unfortunately for these same reasons that many a working dog finds itself without a home or family, and why AWDRI was established.

I first stumbled across the amazing work Carey and Di Edwards have undertaken with AWDRI while surfing Facebook.

After going gaga over the myriad incredibly cute puppy photos, I read between the cute and discovered exactly what this incredible organisation did, rescuing and rehoming thousands of abandoned working dogs every year. I just had to get involved. It's been a wonderful twelve months of work with AWDRI as their ambassador thus far, my job entailing everything from creating awareness of the organisation within the media, securing sponsors, hosting our exhibitions at events such as the Royal Melbourne Show, adoption days, paws in the park events, as well as photography shoots for the yearly calendar, and presenting on *Lateline*.

It is the utmost honour to be involved with such an amazing organisation. Watching them grow daily, seeing the widespread impact they have saving so many furry lives is an absolute joy. I will be a volunteer with AWDRI for life, and deeply thank you for your generosity in purchasing this book to support Australian Working Dog Rescue.

Erin Victoria Holland

Our Dogs

As you'd imagine, our family is 'dog central'! At the time of writing we have five, both working and companion dogs. Here's our story as told through some of the dogs we've cherished over the years.

Bud

We had a little dog, Sparky, who was 15. He was said to be a border collie x Australian terrier but his heritage was a little dubious. Regardless, he was a wonderful dog who went everywhere with us. As he got older we talked about getting another dog after he left us. We didn't want to get one until then as we felt it wouldn't be fair on him, having been an only child his whole life, but we found ourselves going into pet shops (before we knew any better) and looking at puppies anyway.

Then one day our life changed. We walked up to this glass box in a pet shop and in it were three puppies, two brown and white and one black and white. The brown ones were wrestling and playing with each other while the black one sat at the front of the box, stared us in the eye and lifted one paw up as if pleading with us to take him home. We left without him but couldn't stop talking about him. We soon made the decision that if he was still there the next day we would buy him. We named him on the way home that day: his name was to be Bud. I went to work the next morning while Carey went back to the pet shop and got Bud. I walked into the house after work to be greeted by a happy puppy and puppy breath.

Bud has taken us on a steep learning curve as an introduction to working breeds and we wouldn't have it any other way. At time of writing he is $14\frac{1}{2}$ and going strong despite a recent episode of vestibular disease. We hope to have him with us for some time yet. He is just stubborn enough to hang around for years to come just so he can keep the youngsters in line.

Di Edwards

'Bud has taken us on a steep learning curve ... and we wouldn't have it any other way.'

Chip

Where do I start with this dog, who was my everything? We purchased him from a pet shop at 6½ weeks of age to help us and our other dog, Bud, heal from the loss of our dear old boy Sparky, who had died aged 16½.

Chip was my heart and soul. He had many nicknames but his most common was Chippy Monster or just plain Chippy. He started us on the path to rescue by forcing me to join Australian cattle dog forums on the internet to learn more about this breed. Through that, I learned about Australian cattle dog rescue groups in the US and that drove me to do more to help our national working dogs here in Australia. From little seeds do big things grow. AWDRI has Chip to thank for its existence.

He did everything with vim and vigour and adored me above everyone else, and it hurt badly when we found out, when he was only seven, that he was going blind from progressive retinal atrophy complicated by cataracts. Within a year he was totally blind. I still recall the day he couldn't catch a frisbee any more. I cried my heart out, thinking his life of fun was over. But in fact it forced me to think outside the box and find different things to do.

Chip did so many things that even sighted dogs don't get to enjoy. Look up 'Blind Herding' on YouTube and you'll find Chippy chasing the sheep around the round yard. Look up 'Blind Bushwalking' and you'll find Chippy trotting along through the bush right behind Bud, full of confidence even though he couldn't see where he was going. His other senses had expanded to compensate for his lack of vision and he had an incredible radar that detected when obstacles were in his way.

He was the best cuddler and kisser I have ever met; I never had much makeup left after he greeted me on my return from work. Despite having multiple malignant skin cancers removed, he still lived life to its fullest until, just after his eleventh birthday, liver cancer took him from us. May 28 each year is now AWDRI Tribute Day in his honour, a day when we pause to remember the animals who have touched our lives and our hearts.

Di Edwards

Nimble

After the loss of AWDRI Speedy and three of her siblings to parvovirus in early November 2012, a huge hole was left in our hearts and thus the search for the next dog holding the AWDRI name began. Just before Christmas 2012 photos came through of a litter of kelpies surrendered to the organisation in Hervey Bay, Queensland. The litter consisted of six girls and two boys. We were drawn to one little girl with folded back ears and a cheeky look. Thus AWDRI Nimble came into our lives.

Promoting the cause often finds AWDRI at agricultural shows, including country fairs such as the Morisset Show (right). Our dogs demonstrate their wide range of skills, from tricks and training to herding demonstrations and high jump. Nimble is always a crowd favourite.

Carey Edwards

'When Carey said I could keep her, my heart danced inside my chest.'

Tricky

I had no intentions of adopting another dog. I had my hands full with three dogs already including Pudding, my stubborn, challenging red cattle dog bitch, but fate had other things in store for me.

I thought I was driving to Gundagai just to pick up a litter of kelpie pups that another volunteer had collected from the Griffith pound. The pups were to stay with us in quarantine and then either be adopted or placed in other foster homes. Looking back at photos taken that day, she was working her wiles on me from the moment I picked her up out of that crate at the Dog on the Tuckerbox.

I got the pups home and put them in the quarantine pen, and from that moment she did everything she could to keep me in her sight, including climbing between the enclosure wall and barrier and climbing up the wall to sit on the timber barrier. Every time I went out to see them she was the first one jumping up at the barrier with the cheekiest smile you ever saw. She wormed her way into my heart quicker than you can say 'Sucker'!

When Carey came home from his trip away and met the pups, he decided he might keep one of the litter to train up as a worker. That had always been his plan, but I was secretly gutted that I might not be able to keep her because that would take us up to five dogs, and only crazy people have that many dogs!

So when he said I could have her too, my heart danced inside my chest. She is my Tricky Trickster and I absolutely adore her smart attitude, her intelligence and her charming tricks. She loves her big sisters and brother and fits in beautifully, adding another dimension to our pack and to what we, as an organisation, can do.

Di Edwards

'Just because we're on the farm doesn't mean a dog doesn't get to play now and then. Even true working dogs love a game of fetch, and the time to just be dogs.'

The Working Breeds

The Australian working dog breeds in these pages are cattle dogs, kelpies, border collies and koolies. Bred for herding sheep or cattle, these dogs are highly intelligent, have a strong instinct to work and are easily trained. They also make wonderful and loyal companions.

Cattle dog

The Australian cattle dog. The general appearance is that of a strong, compact, symmetrically built working dog, with the ability and willingness to carry out his or her allotted task however arduous.

The combination of power, balance and hard muscular condition conveys the impression of great agility, strength and endurance. The cattle dog's loyalty and protective instincts make it a self-appointed guardian to the stockman, his herd and his property.

Agility, strength and endurance.

Loyalty and devotion to duty.

Kelpie

The Australian kelpie — a lithe, active dog of great quality. It is muscular yet supple of limb and capable of untiring work. The kelpie is extremely alert, eager and highly intelligent, with a mild, obedient disposition and an almost inexhaustible energy, with marked loyalty and devotion to duty. It has a natural instinct and aptitude for the working of sheep, both in open country and in the yard.

Keen, alert and eager.

Border collie

Originally from the Anglo-Scottish border regions, the border collie has found itself very much at home in Australia, where it is widely employed as a working sheep dog. The border collie is a graceful, balanced and well-proportioned dog with sufficient strength to ensure that it is capable of long periods of active duty. The breed is highly intelligent, with an instinctive tendency to work and is readily responsive to training. Its keen, alert and eager expression add to its appearance of intelligence, while its loyal and faithful nature means that it is kindly disposed towards stock.

Koolie

The koolie is as diverse as the country it originates from, Australia. In the north of Queensland and New South Wales they are tall, medium boned and agile, bred for mustering cattle over great distances. In the Hunter Valley and Snowy Mountains regions of New South Wales they're thicker set and shorter, and able to flush cattle from low-lying dense bush and gullies. All koolies are agile, with a great ability to adapt to any situation and a strong willingness to work.

Agile, adaptable and
willing to work.

Getting the kids involved in the fostering process is a great way to teach them about responsibility.

Puppy Power

Who can resist a puppy? But working breed pups are more than a
bundle of cuteness — they are feisty little balls of energy!

Car goes fast.
So do puppies!

To adopt a puppy, simply complete an application on AWDRI's website. There's usually a bit of a waiting list, which is a good thing when you're in the business of saving lives.

Wheelie cute

As a pup, Abbie was small enough to fit into the wheel of a parked car. Abbie came from Townsville into our care in Adelaide, and it wasn't long before she wormed her way into her carer's heart and became a foster fail — a dog whose carer cannot bear to part with it, and becomes the adopter.

Four in hand

Adelaide has become a major rescuing centre, taking in dogs from many far-flung rural towns in several states. These kelpie pups came from Mildura in far western Victoria and are pictured with two of our foster carers and another Australian classic — a Ford Falcon XY GT.

Don't it make your brown eyes ...

Many kelpies are born with blue eyes. Of course this means that they are extremely cute when young, tempting many people to buy a puppy that turns out to be a whirlwind in their backyard. These dogs often wind up in a pound or shelter, which is why we ask people to never buy a dog on a whim or on impulse. Rescue organisations such as AWDRI offer a trial period, so what better way to find your next best friend? Of course, much like wolves, kelpies' eye colour changes as they grow older, usually to a yellow/green/brown colour.

A Gilgandra pup

After being found dumped on the side of the road at Gilgandra in central New South Wales, this three-week old puppy needed a good bath and lots of TLC. Eleven pups in total were found, with two being taken by RSPCA for rehoming and the remaining nine coming to AWDRI. Each of the gorgeous little pups has gone on to a wonderful home and is living an active and happy life.

After fostering several of the Gilgandra pups, Tara Gunter just couldn't resist the charms of this little fellow (right) and kept him to join her crew of working dogs at Calmsley Hill City Farm in western Sydney. Kelpie by name, kelpie by breed and kelpie by nature. He's a spunky, feisty little boy who is loved by his mum even if he is selectively deaf at times.

You looking at me?

Border collie pup at Diggers Rest, Victoria.

This little bluey was dumped in traffic — but has now found his forever home.

Baby blue

Back at the start of April 2014 we were contacted by RSPCA New South Wales to see if we could help with rehoming a young blue cattle dog pup that they had in their shelter in Sydney. The story goes that someone saw a car stop on a major road in one of Sydney's suburbs and drop a pup out of the car and drive off. The pup wandered into the traffic but fortunately some people stopped to save it. It turned out the pup was deaf, which is probably why he had been dumped. We took him into foster care at AWDRI HQ and he spent Easter with the crew before finding his forever home with a wonderful family on 200 acres with another couple of cattle dogs as siblings.

The Wookies

Chewy (left) and her siblings were surrendered to us in December 2014. Kelpie x wolfhound, they are quite striking in appearance, and are all friendly, with beautiful natures. Nicknamed 'Wookies' because of their resemblance to the creature in *Star Wars*, Chewy was named after Chewbacca, Han Solo's offsider.

'Chooey the internet sensation!'

Chooey, internet star

Rescued from the Narrandera pound in southern New South Wales, Chooey was fostered at AWDRI HQ, where she became a internet sensation after being photographed sleeping on the back of our sheep. This photo has been shared on just about every site on the net, including the Huffington Post and BuzzFeed. An adorable little cattle dog pup, she was adopted by a wonderful family on a property in Queensland, and now has three other cattle dog sisters to play with.

Nimble shows off her tail end.

True Calling

Working dogs have a natural instinct for herding, which makes them invaluable on rural properties throughout Australia. But even urban dogs can develop their natural instincts through training programs in which both dog and owner learn new skills and strengthen their bond.

'For our organisation, this was a true victory.'

Rex, the $4250 dog

Rex was the catalyst for AWDRI's association with Steve Sudero and his Yarra Valley Working Dog program. Rex's original owner had been unable to train him to work and Rex had subsequently spent around seven months of his life tied to a tree. He was due to be euthanased, but the vet practice contacted AWDRI to see if we could take him in, which we did.

Steve knew that Rex came from a long line of great working dogs, and had the papers to prove it, so he was keen to give Rex a shot at working life. Over the next seven months Steve trained Rex to a point where he was ready to be the first working dog that AWDRI took to a working dog auction (the Casterton auction, held every year during the town's kelpie festival).

Rex ended up fetching $4250, and as far as anyone knows, holds the world record for the sale price of a rescue dog, either at auction or otherwise. Rex, being of the blood lines he is, was not de-sexed (as nearly all rescues are) so he can not only work as he was bred to do, but can add to the gene pool for future generations.

Rex went to a farm where he works in excess of 4000 head of sheep. For our organisation, this was a true victory.

Basic instinct

Many of the dogs that come to AWDRI go with their foster carers to sheep-herding classes to test their instincts. The city dog sometimes finds that sheep herding is just the activity it was born to do. A first-timer, such as in this photo, can show such a talent for moving stock that people assume they have been doing it for years.

Doin' what comes naturally

In some regions of the country working dog puppies are introduced to stock at quite an early age. Some show great instincts for work at just six weeks old. A dog moving to the lead animal at the head of the stock is always a good sign of working potential, and some pups just do it naturally, like this little girl.

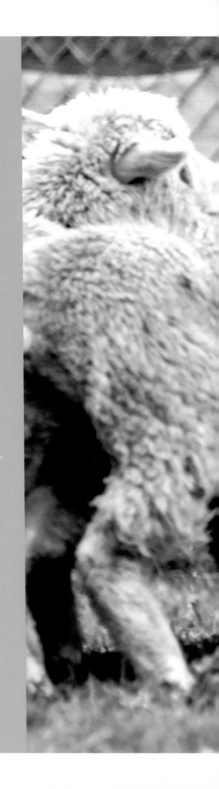

Balancing act

The object of a gathering dog, such as the kelpie, is to 'balance' the sheep to the handler. This means that if the handler is in the 12 o'clock position, the dog is in the 6 o'clock position, and the livestock (typically sheep) are in the centre of the dial. Wherever the handler moves, be that on foot, on horseback, or quad bike, the dog moves in such a manner that the sheep stay in the middle of the dial, and the dog stays in the 6 o'clock position. A good dog can also work 'off balance' as it matures and better understands the handler's instructions.

Don't box me in

The eyes have it. This working pup is keenly waiting its turn on the sheep. Once that instinct kicks in there is no turning back — they just want to work.

Calmsley Hill City Farm

Calmsley Hill City Farm in western Sydney is a working farm of some 80 hectares. It is an educational facility where children and adults can enjoy a variety of shows and exhibits involving farm animals and native wildlife. The staff foster and care for many AWDRI dogs, including whole litters that have been surrendered or dumped, and several of the staff have adopted AWDRI dogs. Tara, the farm manager, works closely with all the dogs, and has several rescues of her own, including Rusty (left, in the foreground) who was handed in to the farm as an owner surrender. Rusty and the other dogs on the farm work the other animals as required, and give working dog demonstration each day for the visitors.

Crowds of people watch daily sheep-shearing demonstrations at the farm, and are usually joined by an AWDRI dog or two as well. In the photo to the right Chilli — a little kelpie x New Zealand huntaway — has taken to the stage.

Jess and Chilli

Chilli is a kelpie x New Zealand huntaway who was rescued from the Hawkesbury pound. She's proved her real worth with her owner Jess at Calmsley Hill City Farm, where she does daily working dog demonstrations with sheep. Her friendly and gentle disposition means that bus-loads of kids feel confident in patting and playing with her.

The paws that refreshes

Not every dog wants to work in the sun all day long. After doing the daily sheep-herding demonstration at Calmsley Hill City Farm, Dot takes a moment to cool off while Simone talks to the audience about the dogs' role on the farm.

Trainer Paul Macphail brings out
the best in working dogs.

Beloka Kelpie Stud

Paul Macphail of Beloka Kelpies is a working dog trainer and great friend of AWDRI. As well as taking in many of AWDRI's rescues and retraining them, Paul also holds dog schools which help our carers and volunteers become better dog handlers. Among his own working crew is a rescue, proving that some dogs are just made for certain lifestyles. As any tradesman will tell you, you need 'the right tool for the job', and Paul's ability to work out what job a dog is made for is what makes him such a great handler and trainer.

Woolly-minded

You can nearly always find one or two farm dogs hanging around the woolshed after crutching. Some like the smells, others like the comfort factor. The rescue dogs Paul Macphail takes in at the Beloka Kelpie Stud get to experience all parts of the farm. The experiences are all part of the training and socialisation needed to produce a great dog.

Waiting his turn

William (foreground) waits patiently for his turn on the sheep. Working dogs must learn to wait when told, and are often kept on short chains to teach them that patience. Just one unruly dog who won't wait can panic a lot of livestock and cause stress, so this part of the training is crucial for farmers who want to move stock around the farm and to market in the best possible condition.

Beloka dogs in action

Working five dogs simultaneously might be a pipe dream for some, but for others, like Paul Macphail, it's a way of life.

Herding requires numerous
obedience skills.

Diggers Herding

At Diggers Herding, on the north-western outskirts of Melbourne, urban herding enthusiasts and their dogs learn how to round up sheep. Owners David Higgins and Geoff Burling look after many AWDRI dogs, foster carers and adopters, as well as dog-owning members of the general public.

Many of the dogs attending Diggers Herding (and several similar facilities around the country) have 'dropped out' of typical dog obedience classes, which generally cater to breeds without the energy levels of a working dog. Herding sheep requires numerous obedience skills, along with an understanding of how stock move, and a great bond with your owner.

It's no surprise then that it is a favourite way for many people to spend time with their working dog, and that it ultimately leads to a fantastic relationship with their dog, and a much better behaved and trained dog.

Indi was perfect from the moment she joined Jeff's family.

Jeff and Indi

Indi came to Jeff after first meeting Nimble and Carey at the Beloka Easter trials in 2014. Jeff left Beloka that day knowing that he 'really did want a kelpie, and it was going to be a Black and Tan'.

In the following months Jeff applied to adopt and came to meet Indi, a dog who had been surrendered into the care of AWDRI due to the ill-health of the previous owner. Indi was perfect from the moment she joined Jeff's family. Her obedience, recall and enthusiasm for life was abundant. Life was a big game.

Jeff attended working dog schools at Beloka, and brought his level of dogmanship up a few notches to better understand and work with Indi — a sign of a truly dedicated owner.

Sadly, on the last weekend of March 2015, Indi was lost to this world, which devastated Jeff and his family. Jeff has pledged to foster in the future and help save more lives.

Learning the trade

Rescued from a pound in northern Victoria, this border collie is learning the basics of sheep herding at Diggers Herding.

One of the senior
residents at Diggers
Herding, Rosie, chills out
when the herding classes
are in full swing.

While waiting for a turn at sheep-herding classes, enthusiasts push to the front for a better look.

Lorelle and Pete

Lorelle writes: Pete was my third foster for AWDRI. He came from the Wagga Wagga pound and was cell-mate with another AWDRI dog, so they were either found together, surrendered together, or just got along well enough to be housed in the same pen, which is not common, but if you know Pete, you'll know that's not hard to believe.

I knew nothing about Pete prior to meeting him, apart from that he was a male black and tan kelpie about 12 months old. He was collected by another volunteer from transport and minded for a couple of hours until I finished work and could come and get him. She gave him the name Pete, and, although I never liked it much, and made several attempts to change it, it stuck, and has grown on both of us.

I knew I was in danger of foster failing within the first minute of meeting Pete. He was more like eight or nine months old and full of puppy playfulness; a scrawny, lanky lad with a face with too much black and not enough tan in it for my liking, but it was love at first sight.

I took Pete to Diggers Herding, where David Higgins confirmed that he was probably around eight months old, had potential, but was a bit sensitive and was put off easily by too harsh a word or tone of voice. He posted Pete on his Facebook page to help advertise his availability for adoption. We decided that the ideal home for Pete would probably be one where he could be a part of the family as a pet, but also got to work sheep.

As the days went by, I realised that I wanted to be the person that Pete needed … someone who would give him cuddles, let him play, but also let him work, which is what he loves and lives for. I had to become this person, and so began my journey into the wonderful world of training for, and competing in, sheep dog trials.

Under the tutelage of Steve Sudero from Yarra Valley Working Dogs, I am still learning to be a trial dog handler and Pete rewards me with his amazing growth since we started. From a weak, soft dog, I've seen him grow in confidence before my eyes. My chest swells with pride watching him come into his own — watching and thinking for himself, sensing and working with me (and doing what's right when I tell him to do something wrong!).

I used to think Pete was repaying me for believing in him when no one else did, but now I realise that I'm the one who owes him — a great deal. I am the one who has grown more. It could have been a different dog, a different time, a different foster carer. He could have been more of a pet dog, with little drive or instinct, or too much of a worker for me to handle, but someone up there knew we would make a good team.

I laugh when I hear people say rescue dogs are broken or faulty in some way. Pete is probably the best dog I've ever owned. He is healthy. He has intelligence (obedient and instinctive), perfectly balanced with affection. He loves unconditionally, and unreservedly, despite indications that he was treated cruelly at one point. He puts his trust in me — and that's a big deal. He made me appreciate the hard work and rewards that come with a high-energy, highly focused, smart dog, while still valuing the family-friendly traits of loyalty and affection that I've been used to in dogs since I was just a few weeks old. One that knows me and my moods and loves me just the same … the mark of a true friend. He ticks a lot of boxes, and that's high praise from a perfectionist.

Dodgey at the bar

Even working dogs need downtime after
a hard day's yakka!

Jimmy

In August of 2013 we were contacted by Jimmy's former owner
for assistance in rehoming him. He'd been rejected as a working
dog at three months because he showed no signs of instinct. He
was taken as a pet, but his love of poultry proved a problem, and
thus he came into our care aged almost five months. We tested
him on our sheep and he was a true natural, showing ability
and maturity beyond his age. He proved that you can't always
detect instinct in pups, as some develop this later than others.
After some basic training Jimmy was adopted and now lives as a
working dog with a jackaroo, herding both sheep and cattle. For
our co-founder, Carey, Jimmy is 'the one that got away': he fell
for him but let him go.

Dogs at Work

Not all working dogs follow a traditional path and end up mustering sheep and cattle in the outback. They can also become therapy dogs, mascots and even wine dogs ...

Sahara: Brand ambassador

Sahara (right) is an amazing little koolie kelpie cross that was found wandering outback New South Wales and taken to the Mildura Animal Shelter. She now lives with a gang of other doggy friends at Diggers Herding and K9 Education on the outskirts of Melbourne. She is the ambassador for Jetpets, one of AWDRI's partners, and for all of animal rescue in general. Nimble (left) and Sahara have appeared together in events to promote rescue and responsible dog ownership.

'Ranger is the most wonderfully quirky dog!'

Sharon and Ranger

Sharon writes: Ranger is currently six months old, and is now a wine and cellar door dog living at a five-star winery and vineyard in the Adelaide Hills. We adopted Ranger from AWDRI after little Sheldon (his brother) sadly died before we could adopt him. We were devastated, but a week later we adopted Ranger and hope that Sheldon is looking down on him, happy that Ranger has the most wonderful life. He is the most wonderfully quirky dog and loves posing for the camera. We love that he often has one stuck up big ear and one that is folded; he is very cute and his spots are amazing.

Carolyne and George

Foster carer Carolyne Cousins runs a furniture restoration business on one side of her property in southern Victoria. George is the original working resident who likes to hang around the shop, and also has an affinity for the family's pet pig, whom he follows around whenever he's roaming the yard.

Three classics

Jodi, AWDRI's South Australian co-ordinator, runs a business restoring classic cars with her husband. This gives some of our dogs the opportunity to mix with something nearly as fast as they are.

Two girls and two boys. The Stone sisters spend a lot of time with Finn (left) and Alfie at the local beach.

The Stone family and Finn

Lyn writes: When it came time for us to have a dog, we knew we wanted a rescue. Pound after pound was scoured for months, and although we didn't find the right dog, we came closer to realising what our ideal was. It was this search that led us to AWDRI and eventually to Finnigan.

Yarra Valley Working Dogs had taken him on after he was found wandering the streets in Taree. Unfortunately, he wasn't suited to working with stock: his idea of work was running in circles barking. But that disadvantage turned into a massive plus for us.

Finnigan is the most loving, goofy, good-natured and wonderful animal I have ever had in my life. Where before we had pets, Finnigan is family. He knows not to lick or knock my disabled daughter. He gives unconditional love to everyone he meets. He is faithful, obedient and just really really silly. He does something that makes you laugh every day.

He is so calming and serene that I decided to have him assessed as a Delta Therapy Dog. He passed with flying colours, and now each fortnight we visit a local aged care facility.

Finn isn't doing a 'working dog' job, but bringing smiles to the faces of the residents, and indeed everyone he meets, is what he's cut out to do.

He has brought more happiness into existence in his few years on Earth than some do in a lifetime.

He also smells fantastic, like chocolate biscuits crushed into a carpet. He is an angel.

Ruth: Army recruit

Ryan is a dog handler in the army and fosters our difficult dogs and rehabilitates them using the skills he has learned through his job. Ruth, in this photo with Ryan, is his working dog.

Coach & Kip: Wine dogs

In the rescue community there are so many people with kind hearts. One such person is Adam Castagna of Castagna Vineyard in Beechworth, Victoria. As with most vineyards and wineries, dogs are part of the family. Coach (left), a red cattle dog, was found alone in the bush aged about four weeks, while Kip, the wolfhound cross, was adopted from another rescue organisation.

Fosters
(and foster fails)

AWDRI relies on our wonderful volunteers, including a network of dedicated
foster carers who'll care for and rehabilitate their charges until they are ready
to find their 'forever' homes. But sometimes the foster carer falls for the dog —
these are our foster 'fails'; failures to be celebrated!

Carolyn and friends

The Fitzsimmons family from outside Bendigo in Victoria have been a large part of AWDRI's rescue operations for several years now, with Carolyn (on left) having held the role of Victorian adoptions co-ordinator for most of those years. Carolyn now occupies the role of adoptions manager, advising and guiding AWDRI's adoptions co-ordinators in each state. Pictured with Carolyn on the daily early-morning rabbit chasing expedition are a few family members, including Skye (daughter), Rooney the fawn kelpie, one of the many foster dogs that come to visit, and Daphne the deaf cattle dog.

Diesel is Jodi's shadow and her best mate.

Diesel

Diesel was one of six puppies rescued from a rural area and transferred to foster care in South Australia.

Three pups of the litter, including Diesel, became critically ill with parvovirus — a terrible affliction for puppies to have.

After surviving his first few weeks of treatment, Diesel came into the care of Jodi, one of AWDRI's South Australian co-ordinators. Diesel was a fantastic little pup who fitted in immediately with Jodi's other two dogs, a 12-month-old female kelpie, Pip, and 14-year-old staffy, Tyler.

After Diesel's potential adopter didn't work out, Jodi's family decided they could not part with him and applied to adopt him … Diesel was meant to be theirs.

Having reached Level 4 obedience by 12 months of age, they can't wait to see what Diesel can achieve in the next few years. He is Jodi's shadow. Her best mate. Diesel was a foster brother, teacher and companion to five dogs in 2014, each one a part of Jodi's family until they have found their own.

Wayne and Jock

Many of the people who foster and volunteer for AWDRI not only help save the lives of dogs, but volunteer for other community organisations. Wayne Aumann volunteers for the Country Fire Authority, a volunteer community-based fire and emergency services organisation that helps protect 3.3 million Victorians, and more than one million homes and properties across the state.

Wayne chooses to not keep any dogs on a permanent basis, preferring to continually foster dogs taken off death row, and save as many lives as he can. This is Jock, who was saved from the Wagga Wagga pound in New South Wales.

Ben and Ralph at
Punt Road Oval
— the home of the
Richmond Tigers

Ben and Ralph

Richmond AFL footballer Ben Griffiths came onboard as a foster carer and volunteer as part of the club's program to give their young stars a life outside of the game. Ben's first foster dog, Ralph, came from Mildura pound, and Ben quickly learnt, as so many have before him, that giving a foster dog up can be hard. Very hard. Ben adopted Ralph, and is learning to work stock with him. Ralph is currently AWDRI's highest-jumping dog, with a personal best of 2.55 metres. At the 2014 Royal Melbourne Show Ralph just missed out on scaling 2.7 metres, which would have set him up for a shot at the official world record.

AWDRI ambassador Lauren Vickers

Lauren became involved with AWDRI through her love of dogs and her desire to help save lives. Her experience in the modelling industry has given her a passion for quality in everything she does and her assistance with promoting AWDRI and our dogs in need has been an invaluable addition to the team. Bear, the blue cattle dog, was born with swimmer puppy syndrome which meant his hips were splayed outwards and he was not able to weight-bear at all. Physio and exercise has built him up into the big, strong boy he now is. Ella, the kelpie, is the proud mother of several of the pups featured elsewhere in this book.

CFA carers

All dressed up and waiting for somewhere to go. That's the life of a rescue dog waiting for its forever home. Foster carers give their time to rescue, rehabilitate and then rehome the dogs that come to them. The foster care process has proven to be the best way to prepare dogs for new homes. Because their rehabilitation takes place around a family home, all the unwanted behaviours that led to the dog ending up in a pound or shelter are addressed and corrected.

Cherise: Buddy and Abbie

Cherise with Buddy and Abbie (on right) know who's the fastest here! Since this photo was taken Abbie has gone from foster dog to foster fail, as so many in the rescue industry do.

'Bodhi managed to steal our hearts.'

Toneya and Bodhi

Donna writes: Bodhi (on the right) came into our care for one night only, having been transported from a rural location for surgery on a broken leg. Following surgery the vet recommended he remain with us for six more weeks so that he had easy access to medical care during his recovery. The time was extended after Bodhi decided his first plaster cast was a chew toy, and needed a steel-reinforced replacement.

During this time Bodhi managed to steal our hearts. He spent hours cuddling with Toneya and lying with her, and he would dance with excitement when she finished school. Bodhi's crazy kelpie energy was infectious, and we had to admit that we had 'failed' as foster carers, as we couldn't part with him. Bodhi has been with us now for 12 months, and Toneya continues to be his favourite girl.

Stevie

Stevie is a blue female cattle dog (aka blue heeler) who came from West Wyalong in New South Wales. Entering the home of her foster carers in Victoria, she soon made it her own, and the family joined the famous 'foster fail' club.

The most patriotic of Melbourne's famous Brighton Beach bathing boxes makes a great backdrop for the classic Australian cattle dog.

Tracey and Buddy

Tracey writes: I was Buddy's third foster carer and I think he came from the Hawkesbury pound at five months. He needed a foster home where the other dogs wouldn't pick on him, as he was quite docile. Not a dog or breed I thought I would ever be interested in adopting, but he is a very loving, affectionate and loyal dog.

Someone in our dog walking group was interested in him and he went on trial with them for a week. He was there five minutes and stole their lunch off the kitchen bench! We really missed him, and Cookie (not shown) seemed to as well, as he was her playmate. He was returned, as one of their dogs was not happy with a third dog and it didn't work out.

I realised he had been in at least five homes in eight months and it was time for him to find a permanent one — which was ours. The first night back seemed to confirm this, with Cookie and Buddy snuggled up together in front of the heater.

He has certainly come out of his shell since being with us and we continue to work with him on some naughty behaviours that need, shall we say, modification! And yes, he will still steal food off the kitchen bench if given a chance. Also, he has been the only dog to figure out how to flip the garbage bin open in the kitchen and steal from that as well.

Hamish when he was a puppy.

Leonie and Hamish

Leonie writes: The first thing I did as an AWDRI volunteer was transport Hamish from a carer in Sydney to another carer in Mudgee. During that five-hour trip I fell in love with him, and ended up adopting him. Some carers are 'failed fosters'; I am a 'failed transport'.

I believe Hamish came into AWDRI's care after being found on the side of a road at Gundagai when he was about six weeks old.

Hamish is a cream kelpie, I often get asked if he is a dingo. I sometimes cheekily reply 'yes'.

Mad Baxter

Baxter was one of our early rescues and was in terrible shape when pulled from the Wagga Wagga pound. Emaciated, and suffering with vomiting and diarrhoea and a fungal infection of all his toenails, he was a sorry sight. After temporary care by a local volunteer, he was transferred into foster care with Samantha, who continued his rehabilitation while Baxter dug his way into her heart so deep that she just couldn't let him go. In this photo, Samantha and Baxter re-enact an iconic scene from *Mad Max*.

Scruffy proved to be the perfect dog for one Geelong family.

Scruffy

Scruffy was saved from the Korumburra pound in Victoria. He was surrendered with his sister because his owners were moving into a rental property and couldn't take them.

A family in Geelong agreed to foster Scruffy and picked him up. They started to fall for the little guy even before they had returned home.

When they got home Scruffy jumped out of the car and gave the family's mum the most gentle hug. No discussion needed, this dog had found his forever home.

He is the perfect dog for the family. Gentle, loyal and very much part of their everyday life.

Peri and friends

Peri and two of her fosters pose outside the festival grounds at Deniliquin, where every October the air is filled with the sounds of thousands of utes attending the Deni Ute Muster.

Deni sunset

Foster carer, adopter, transporter. Just some of the things Peri Chappell is and does from her base in Deniliquin, a country town in the Riverina region of New South Wales.

Sharyn and Summer

Summer was captured as a stray and impounded at the West Wyalong pound in New South Wales. Nobody claimed her, but the ranger held her for six weeks, unable to give up on her due to her lovely nature. Sharyn was asked to give her temporary care and she takes up the story.

I met her at Diggers Herding and wow, what a dog. She was stunning; all kelpie.

She'd recently had a litter, and apparently had been found on the street with a puppy, but the rangers thought it wasn't hers because it didn't look anything like her.

So the plan was to move her quickly, as soon as another carer became available, because I had my hands full with several other dogs at the time. I had a friend take professional photographs the day after she arrived. But later that weekend we went to an AWDRI fundraiser BBQ. In the rain she was so well behaved, and she just looked up at me as if to say 'Will you be my mummy?'

Everyone said she adored me. I realised later that she was that way with everyone!

She understood English, I swear to God. She was good with my dear old Ernie. They were playing rough one day and I leant out the door and said, 'Heh... He's an old man; go easy on him.' So she got down on her belly and played low. OMG bless.

Then when AWDRI Tippy arrived Summer lay down beside her and told her not to be scared, you're safe now, you can sleep. And she did. Tippy hadn't slept the whole time in the pound as she was so scared and shut down. Summer was her rock. When I lost Ernie to cancer she took over his role and taught the newbies not to be scared.

I have never seen anything like this dog. She's intuitive, good with oldies and children; tough but snugly. She is utterly brilliant on sheep! I've had to relearn! I just couldn't give her away. She belonged here, and here she has stayed as a forever sister to Tippy, a blue Australian cattle dog, and Molly, a short-haired border collie.

Tania and Widget

Widget was a small pup from West Wyalong in New South Wales fostered by Tania Quinlan. Now she's her foster fail and is often described as a 'western suburbs miniature kelpie', and where else should a western suburbs dog go but to the Whitten Oval, in Footscray, Melbourne.

Grace by name and Grace by nature...

Every life is precious

Grace is a beautiful fawn kelpie who was given up to the Geelong Animal Welfare Society (GAWS). Initially Grace was supposed to be the first foster dog of new AWDRI volunteer Viv Cullen, but, in her words 'I just could not let her go.'

Grace's story is typical of many dogs AWDRI comes to care for. It is assumed that Grace was given up because of undesired working traits, as she has clearly worked in the past.

It has taken some time for her to trust her surroundings, and only she knows what her life was like previously. She has been to Diggers K9 Education to play with some sheep, which she enjoyed (once she realised her family wouldn't be yelling at her), and it helped to bring her out of her shell a little. She is still very timid, but becoming more trusting every day. Viv and everyone who worked with Grace at GAWS is enamoured of her. She is a very special dog.

'Rosie is my little sidekick!'

Kristy and Rosie

Kristy writes: Rosie was a failed foster with AWDRI. She came from the Muswellbrook pound at about 16 weeks and after a few weeks we started noticing her tripping over things and bumping into stuff. A visit to the eye vet confirmed that she had detached retinas and we were told she would be completely blind by 18 months. She's five in April and has only just in the past few months gotten worse. She does very well, though. I was very naive and thought no one would want a blind dog and it would be better to adopt her, as she was used to her surroundings, so I did (I know now someone would have wanted her), but I'm so happy she stayed. She is my little sidekick and I love her with all my heart, vision or no vision.

Happy Ever After

This is why we're in the rescue business: the joy and satisfaction of helping abandoned dogs find the love and security of a forever home ...

Jason and Miff

Naughty Puppy Miff! After lasting only a couple of hours at her first adoptee home, Miff was packed up and returned to her foster carer. When Jason read this news on the AWDRI Facebook page he was curious. He enquired as to who this puppy was and asked for a photo. Jason takes up the story.

As soon as I saw the photo, that was it. Naughty Puppy Miff was also a heart stealer. I completed all the paperwork and before I knew it she was flying down from Brisbane to Mildura, where I was to meet her for the very first time.

Miff's arrival was delayed as the flight crew had forgotten to put her on her scheduled flight. She was put on the next flight and arrived in Mildura at 8.30 in the evening rather than at 3.30 in the afternoon. It was a very long wait, as I was super excited to be meeting our new puppy.

I was in the terminal when Miff arrived. The plane had landed and the engines were shut down and I could hear this terrible shrieking bark. Yep, that was Miff, protesting about her late delivery. She continued to bark while she was being unloaded, right until she was in my arms after being signed for in the freight shed.

The freight handler told me that she should have come with a box of earplugs, as she barked and annoyed every passenger for the whole flight.

'Rocky was our first ever rescue
from Cairns, our home town.'

Rocky #1

Rocky was our first ever rescue from the Cairns pound in north Queensland. Despite having been founded in Cairns, most of our rescues were from New South Wales and south east Queensland, so it was quite a milestone to be able to save a dog in our backyard. Lacking any foster carers in the area, Rocky was boarded at a local shelter, where he had to be placed into quarantine because of kennel cough. While in boarding we received an application to adopt him from a family on a working property in central Queensland, so as soon as his health was good he flew off to his new family to live happily ever after.

Megan and Otis

Megan writes: I fostered a few dogs for AWDRI and on one occasion spotted a beautiful brown kelpie while checking the local pounds online. From the moment I saw Otis' picture, I knew I was in love, and that there was no way in this world he was going to be euthanased. It was one of those moments where you tell yourself, 'I just have a really good feeling about this thing.' Sure enough, I was already on my way to pick him up before I could have any second thoughts.

When I arrived, I was taken to meet the shyest dog I had ever encountered. He was friendly enough, but not at all trusting. I popped his lead on and we walked to my car. I could tell he wanted to get closer to me but was terrified about the potential consequences. Otis was quite overweight and in need of a good bath, brush and cuddle. He jumped into my car hesitantly and stared at me, turning the other way when I'd make eye contact. The rest of the car trip home he looked out the window, worried about where he was off to. For the first few car rides to follow, he'd turn and face the seat with his nose pressed against it, eyes wide open — he had no idea about the joys of a good car ride, and I have to admit, it made me chuckle.

For a couple of months he was constantly scared. All you'd have to do was say hello and he'd drop to the floor trembling. He'd slide on his face because he felt safer when he was closer to the ground, almost as if we would hurt him if he dared to sit up straight. There is no doubt in my mind that he was abused before we got him.

I'd sit there for hours outside, brushing him and singing to him. Otis obviously had no clue what 'playing' was — you'd pick up a ball and he'd cower in terror. He was also scared of water and pretty much anyone who looked at him. Initially, I would take him to the local supermarket and stand out the front letting people pet him until he decided they were okay and began letting go of his fear of humans.

It took some time, but I started rewarding him when he showed an interest in playing, until he began to do it for the love of it. People starting remarking about how he'd become a 'real dog' — I remember being shocked the first time I heard him bark out of excitement.

Since then, he has turned around completely, even though he has a few funny quirks. He wags his tail almost constantly, he barks, he fetches, runs faster than a rocket, cuddles people without a second thought, swims, and is so much more confident. I have enjoyed watching him grow into the beautiful dog I could see from day one. He has the greatest smile and gives the BEST cuddles. My cat loves him, my family love him, my housemates love him and most importantly, he loves all of us.

Minnie exploring the Perry
Sandhills near Wentworth,
New South Wales.

Samantha and Minnie

Flashback to November 2012 when we spotted a pitiful sight in the Hawkesbury pound in Sydney: a large mix-breed girl with black hair, what there was of it, and in terrible shape but with the most amazing face with eyes that just glowed. She just begged to be saved, even though she did not exactly fit our criteria of having working breeds in her genes. We don't discriminate against the truly needy.

The pound told us that her alopecia (hair loss) was possibly hormone related but that was all we knew. Upon meeting her we suspected that she might be pregnant, hence the hormonal imbalance, and our vet confirmed it. With her poor condition and her terrible skin with barely any hair, it was deemed to be in her best interest to abort her pups, who were very young, to allow Minnie to recover, as we did not know how bad she would get if the pregnancy were to proceed.

Once she was desexed we discovered just how skinny she really was and how much work she needed to get back to a healthy state. Placed into a loving foster home, she was treated to baths and massages with creams to stimulate hair growth and to reduce the greasiness of her skin. Over this time her beautiful nature really came to the fore and when we had to move her to a second foster family she wormed her way into their hearts and they had no choice but to keep her. She is a different dog now with a full coat of hair that shines in the sun. Those gorgeous glowing eyes remain the same, though, and her joy emanates from within.

'The kids treated Merle like one of the pack.'

Suvi and Merle

Merle was from a rural pound in north Queensland. Being deaf, she was proving a difficult dog to rehome, so the pound asked if we could take her into foster care. When she came to us she was timid and fearful, and would urinate and cower at the sight of an adult. Yet she was very attached to her foster carer's young daughter, Suvi (in photo). She followed the children and slept as close to Suvi as she could. Suvi taught Merle to walk on a lead and Merle started following what Suvi did. We think Merle assumed she was one of the kids. Merle came around in leaps and bounds with the kids treating her like one of the pack. Merle started to learn signs and an adopter came forward who was well educated in sign for animals and humans, so it was decided they would be perfect for Merle.

'He is such an important part
of our family.'

Costa and Bear

Costa writes: Bear was born in Townsville, Queensland, and he was taken to the vet at two weeks of age to be euthanased as he was born with swimmer puppy syndrome. The vet nurse asked if she could try to rehabilitate him rather than see him put him down. With lots of hard work and commitment from his carer,

Bear was able to walk properly, although with a little hip swagger.

We adopted him and he was flown to Newcastle to join us. He is such an important member of our family and is a bundle of energy. This week he finally got the courage to swim in one of the dams. It was a very proud moment for all of us.

Shenzi

In May 2014 one of our volunteers was visiting the Griffith pound to collect a dog for us and noticed a male koolie who had just been impounded. She took a photo and sent it to us, saying she could transport him to Sydney if we could find a carer. Koolies are pretty easy to get carers for due to their unique looks, intelligence and friendliness, and we had no trouble lining up a foster home for him to go to. However, in transit and overnight care it was discovered that he had little apparent bladder or bowel control and had a wound on his abdomen and bruising to his scrotal area. Our vet, Dr Tom Lonsdale, had a look at him the next day but the news wasn't great. Shenzi (as he was now named) was found to have suffered trauma to his groin, tail and nerves in the spinal region. It seemed that someone had injured Shenzi.

Over the next week he slowly improved, on a raw diet, to the point that his stools were solid with no further diarrhoea. But with no indication of returning sensation to his tail we were faced with the possibility of having to amputate it to avoid soiling.

At this time Shenzi was examined by neurological specialist, Dr Georgina Child. The news was both good and bad. Georgina confirmed that the trauma had damaged the nerves in his sacrum, which branch out to the tail and into the bladder and sphincter. While there was some possibility of a return of sensation there were no guarantees. As for amputating the tail, it was decided to take a wait-and-see approach and leave it to Shenzi to show us whether this was warranted or not.

Due to frequent updates on our Facebook page Shenzi had quite a devoted following among our supporters and we did get expressions of interest in adopting him even with his issues. It was fate, though, that his special person was already in his life, having nursed him at the vet clinic and taken him on outings. Since being adopted he has gone from strength to strength, learning to control his bladder and bowel, and even getting some sensation back in his tail. He is a very happy and healthy boy and is loved very much by his family.

More can be learned about Shenzi, his past, and his new life on his own Facebook page.

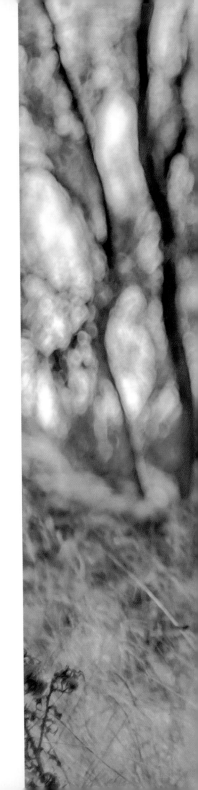

Neda writes: I adopted Luna (the dog on the left) in November last year through AWDRI. I also have Tess, another rescue Australian cattle dog x whippet that we got from Keysborough Animal Shelter (on the right). After getting Luna I fell for AWDRI — hook, line and sinker — and am now a part of the admin team. Luna is my best friend and Tess's best friend. I couldn't have asked for anything more.

The *Cobba* is a paddleboat operating out of Cobram in the north of Victoria along the Murray River. Boofred and Pearl are lucky enough to regularly walk the river with their owner Melissa. Both dogs have complete heterochromia, meaning that one iris is a different colour from the other (usually one brown and one blue). This feature is associated with the Merle gene, which both border collies and koolies carry.

Alby on the rocks

Bells Beach in Victoria is the home of the world's longest-running surfing competition and a favourite place to hang out for a couple of AWDRI dogs and their owners.

Glenn and Bandit

Glenn (with the surfboard) adopted two dogs from AWDRI when the organisation was swamped with seventeen puppies from three separate litters. The puppies were aged between six and eight weeks old at the time of their surrender. Bandit, who is also in the picture with Glenn, was adopted out to another family, but then succumbed to hip dysplasia. His adoptive family could not afford the necessary treatment so it was arranged for Bandit to come back into AWDRI's care. Meanwhile an appeal was run to raise the funds to get Bandit his operation so he could live pain free.

Glenn turned out to be typical of so many of AWDRI's carers — he felt he could not let Bandit go to another home after rehabilitating him, so Bandit was reunited with Buster, another of the seventeen puppies Glenn had already adopted.

Ella and her pups

Ella was rescued from RSPCA New South Wales along with her seven three-day-old puppies, born in the shelter. Ella was fostered by Jenny on the New South Wales Central Coast. Five of the pups were adopted locally so they were able to have their 12-month-reunion at the Norah Head Lighthouse Reserve — they plan to have annual reunions in the future. From left to right: Hunter, Ella, Stella, Ned and Jaffa. (With thanks to NHLR Trust — www.norahheadlighthouse.com.au)

'We take our hat off to owner Bill for the amazing change he has wrought in William.'

Bill and William

Impounded at Wagga Wagga, William was not a happy chap. Scared and timid, he was on the kill list and out of time. Saved by AWDRI, he went into foster care and began to bloom, but it wasn't until he was adopted by Bill that he really started to show his true colours. A challenge from the beginning, being a fear biter, Bill had his work cut out for him, but he stuck with it, training and socialising William and providing him with a loving, stable home. Bill now enters herding trials with William, who shows true instinct and ability. We take our hat off to Bill for the change he has wrought in William and for taking up the challenge and winning. If only all dog owners were like Bill.

Fallon and family

Rescued from the Wagga Wagga pound in late August 2014, Fallon was a sorry sight. Very underweight, with infected ears, a sore eye, cigarette burns over his body and suffering from vomiting and diarrhoea, he was not a well boy (see overleaf).

Taken to the vet he was diagnosed with haemorrhagic gastroenteritis — a very serious condition that many dogs do not survive. Weighing only 12 kilograms, he did not have much in the way of reserves to fight this disease. Despite this he lived up to his name, 'Fallon', which means 'fighter'. Eight days after his admission to the vet he was discharged. He was still fragile and requiring checkups every day.

With lots of TLC and good food he continued his slow recovery.

Then we got some bad news. As he improved and his level of activity increased, we discovered that he had quite an abnormal gait, lifting his back leg when running and not weight-bearing. X-rays revealed that at some point he had suffered a serious break in his femur with the bone fracturing along its length while the head of the femur was still in the hip joint. Surgery was required but he was still very frail and it was four weeks before he had put on enough weight for the operation to proceed.

Despite some further setbacks, he continued to improve in both health and physical activity, and then it was time to write his profile, a task that proved very difficult for his foster mum, who had grown very attached to him throughout his ordeals. He had a few applications but we were on the lookout for that special family who was prepared to go above and beyond to give him a home. It took a little while, but finally, 4 ½ months after coming into care, a very special application came through from the Davies family who had previously adopted a pup from AWDRI. They drove all the way from the Central Coast of New South Wales to meet Fallon in Victoria. Now that's commitment. Antony tells his story.

We first came across Fallon's story on the AWDRI Facebook page, which we have been following closely since we adopted

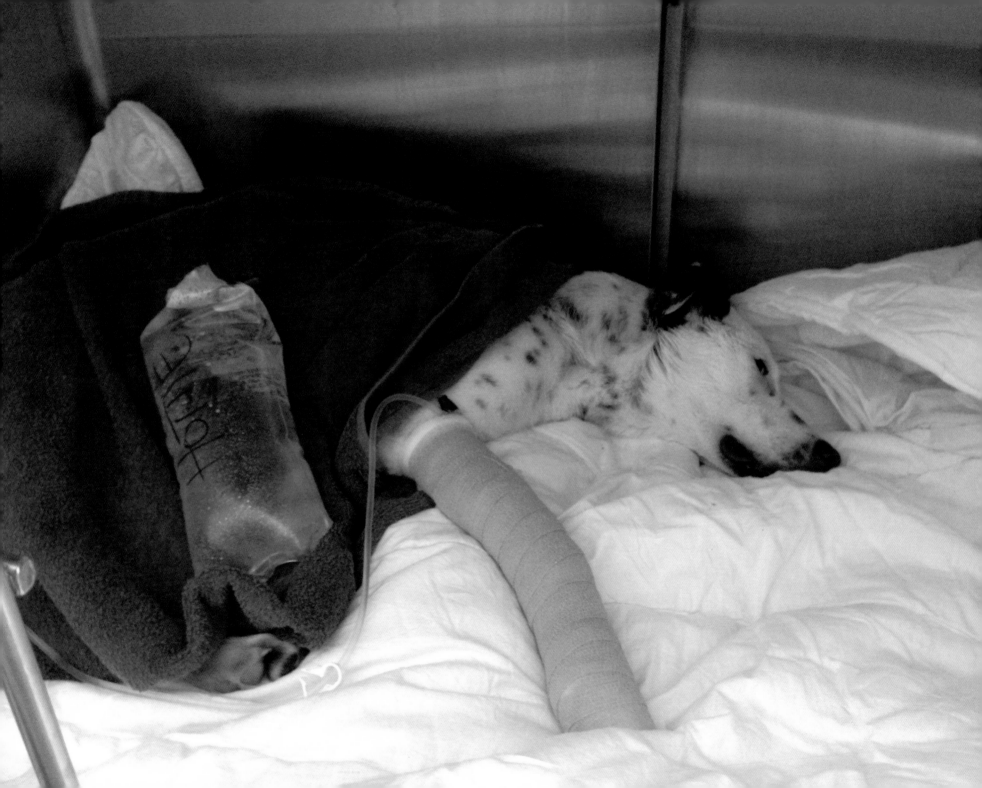

'Fallon has gone from strength to strength.'

our first AWDRI rescue dog, Kozibear. Janel and I have grown up with dogs and believe everybody who is able to should own a dog. They become such a special part of your lives, they are loyal, loving, protective and they bring an insurmountable amount of joy into your life (even after the digging and chewing...). To watch the kids and dogs playing and interacting, exploring and growing together is a pleasure you can't explain if you haven't experienced it.

When we read about Fallon we were heartbroken and disgusted with the treatment and abuse that he had received and it brought Janel to tears on a few occasions.

When we first spoke of putting in our application to adopt him we both concluded that as we already had three dogs, that was enough.

However, the more we read, the more we felt for Fallon. We didn't hear anything for a while and assumed he had been adopted. Then Janel found out he was available and sent me a message saying, 'what's one more to the pack? Let's just apply.' So we did.

After speaking with foster mum Sarah for hours about Fallon's needs and our ability to give him the care he needed we packed ourselves, Mitchell and Kozibear in the car and made the 12 hour trip south.

We met Sarah and Fallon in her local park and Kozibear and Mitchell both fell in love with Fallon instantly, they were running around and wrestling for a couple of hours.

We spent the rest of the day interacting with Fallon and talking about his needs and rehabilitation. We left to have a think about it, but only got about 200 metres down the road before we rang Sarah and said we would like to give it a go.

Fallon has gone from strength to strength and he is such a different dog from when we first got him. He is so happy and full of love after being so mistreated. He is an old soul with a great character and has become a key part of our pack in a short time.

Drew, Skye, Vicki and Daphne

Drew (left) and Skye walk with Vicki (left) who was adopted from Geelong Animal Welfare Society, and Daphne, an owner surrender who is deaf in both ears. Sadly, Vicki passed away in June 2015, aged 13 years.

Sammy and Buca

Owner Sandy writes: Sammy and Buca are litter mates who were dumped in the after-hours pen at Mildura aged approximately six weeks. The pound staff called one of the Victorian co-ordinators for AWDRI, who organised for them to be placed in temporary care. At the time I had just moved into my new house and was looking to adopt a rescue dog. Two weeks later, when they were eight weeks old, I met their carer in Swan Hill and brought them home. I was supposed to adopt one only, but couldn't bring myself to separate them.

'Jaffa is a wonderful addition
to our family.'

Gail and Jaffa

Gail writes: Getting Jaffa happened by accident. I knew there was a litter of kelpie puppies being fostered on the New South Wales Central Coast but deliberately didn't look into it as we weren't looking for a third dog.

I didn't realise at the time that I knew the foster carer, and by total coincidence I saw her on a day when she had them with her at work to keep them cool as it was a 40 degree day. Of course I said yes when she asked if I wanted to have a look; they were four weeks old at the time.

After much thought, we decided the time wasn't right for a puppy. We announced our decision on Facebook, but the foster carer missed the message and I received a text with some cute puppy photos. Tempted, I decided to visit again, put in an application and was lucky enough to get Jaffa.

He is a wonderful addition to our family, and we love him as much as he is loved by his koolie x border collie sister Skye and border collie brother Comet. They are a fantastic trio. Jaffa is following in their paw-steps and will be competing in his first Agility Competition this winter, is training for Obedience, Rally O and Doggy Dancing, and may also have a go at Herding!

CC (aka Cookies and Cream)

CC came to us from the Griffith pound in New South Wales and it wasn't long before she was showing signs of the dreaded parvovirus, endemic in the area she came from, and fatal if not treated early.

Having treated many dogs previously, we decided to nurse CC at home, treating her with a drug called Tamiflu (which kills the virus but cannot undo damage already caused), syringe-feeding her to keep her hydrated and forcing probiotic rich sheep poo down her throat (along with other nutritional supplements). While this is labour intensive and stressful, the reward you feel when the patient turns the corner and starts to eat again is worth every hour of lost sleep.

We are thankful beyond words that she survived and has grown up to be a beautiful dog, now known by the name 'Denali', which means 'the great one' in the native Alaskan Koyukon language.

Tracey and Matt, Gee and Juno

Tracey writes: After I lost my beloved lab, my sister sent me photos of some puppies, hoping I could connect with a rescue and find a companion for our existing dog, Juno. I fell in love with a red cattle dog named Gee immediately and agreed to adopt. I believe we were her fifth home, for many reasons, but we loved her from the first cuddle. Despite a lot of expensive furniture destruction, which was due to separation anxiety, she is an adored member of our family whom we can't imagine not waking up to each day. We thank AWDRI from the bottom of our hearts for the gift of Gigi, as we call her.

Maggie

Maggie is the pride and joy of her adoptive family in Geelong, Victoria. She runs with her mum every day with such joy, and her fearless nature is obvious when she launches herself into the Werribee River. She is everyone's friend and has been easy to train and love.

Justine and Miley

Miley is a red kelpie cross. She is very friendly, but is easily distracted by smells, or if she thinks someone else is having a better time. She is crazy about her ball but only runs around it in clockwise circles.

'Teddy was one of our first purebred greyhound pups.'

Teddy the greyhound

Our co-founder, Di, was visiting a pound one day when a man came in carrying a washing basket holding seven puppies. They appeared to be about three days old. He'd found ten puppies near a railway line. Three of them had perished but he'd taken the other seven home and fed them before bringing them in.

She had no idea what breed they were but Di couldn't leave them there, so she organised foster carers to hand-rear the pups.

Sadly, due to their poor start in life, we lost four of them to malnutrition and failure to thrive, but Teddy here survived, along with his two brothers, Buster and Bear. It was only as they got older that we suspected that they might be greyhounds and a DNA test confirmed it. They were our first purebred greyhound pups and stunning examples they are.

All three are now adopted to wonderful families, and we are very proud of the work all of our carers did in helping them become the healthy, fit animals they are.

Nero loves his new life with
Susan and Ryan.

Susan and Ryan, Nero and Sloan

Nero (left) was born at an RSPCA shelter in December 2012. He was adopted at eight weeks, but returned five months later as a dog who had been left out the back and ignored, not trained, and possibly mistreated.

Nero loves his new life with owners Susan and Ryan and is into obstacles — every time he comes back from a walk he insists on jumping on the letterbox!

Nero has recently become a foster big brother with the help of AWDRI. At the time of our photoshoot he was hosting Sloan, an 11-month-old border collie cross, who was rescued from the pound in Canberra, and who has since been adopted.

Peter and Yardley

It was April 2010 and two dogs came to our attention in the Hawkesbury pound. One was a three-legged blue cattle dog and the other was a brindle and white mix-breed girl. An elderly couple had found them in the bush where they had been dumped and had taken them to the pound. This story touched us deeply, imagining how lost and alone they would have felt, abandoned by those they had loved, scared and not knowing anyone around them. We saved both dogs but sadly, due to the nature of foster care, were unable to place them together.

Around the same time a family from South Australia were holidaying in New South Wales and had applied to adopt a red cattle dog from a pound on the Central Coast. They drove several hours to visit her on the understanding that our organisation had reserved her for them, but unbeknownst to us, or the family, the original rescue organisation that had saved her had claimed her back and given her to another family, rendering their hours of travel useless. They were sorely disappointed, as were we, but they didn't give up.

They went home but contacted us when they saw our three-legged boy and applied to adopt him. At that time we hadn't really named him, but on the way to the airport our volunteer named him Yardley (3 feet to 1 yard) and although the adopters tossed up the idea of calling him Tilt, Yardley kind of stuck. He is very happy, living not far from the beach in Adelaide and is a real daddy's boy.

Paul and Tiggy

Volunteers at a pound in far-western Victoria came into work one morning and found a cardboard box crudely taped shut with a head sticking out of it. The special package had been dropped down the overnight chute during the night. Given the way he was delivered, it was most likely an owner who had dumped him.

When his impound period expired, and he had neither been claimed nor adopted, the dog-in-a-box came into the care of our South Australian co-ordinators. We posted him on our Facebook page and an article featured in the *Sunday Mail* newspaper in Adelaide soon after. Named Tiggy, after a character in the TV series *Sons of Anarchy*, he went from strength to strength and soon found a forever home with his new dad Paul.

Carolynne, Kenny and Pandora

Kenny (right) was rescued from West Wyalong pound back in 2010; he was a scared and skinny little fellow who went into foster care and started on the path to wellness and trust in humans. After some time his adopter, Carolynne, contacted us with a request to adopt a kelpie boy. Having lost their dog not long before, they were missing a dog in the family and Kenny was just what they were looking for so he was flown down to Melbourne and into their hearts. He has not looked back and spends his time lazing on his mum and dad's bed, 'stalking' the family cats and occasionally chasing some sheep around.

Pandora (left) was on death row in the pound in Canberra when Carolynne put her hand up to foster her. A timid girl, she is very friendly and cuddly and loves nothing more than being gently stroked while holding on tight to you. It didn't take long for Carolynne and her family to recognise the bond that had formed between Pandora (now nicknamed Pandy) and Kenny and the love that had built up between her and the rest of the family. Pandy was here to stay.

Rusty is now the happiest of dogs.

Kerrie and Rusty

In September 2014 RSPCA New South Wales contacted AWDRI seeking assistance with placing Rusty in a foster home. He had been seized after CCTV footage came to light showing his previous owner bashing him in an apartment block lift. Investigations revealed multiple, repeated such instances of abuse. Due to his past treatment he had to be medicated to control his anxiety and stress, but despite all this he kept his love and trust in humans and never displayed any aggression whatsoever.

After posting Rusty's story on our Facebook page we found a carer in Victoria who was able to take him in and help him through his rehabilitation. After a couple of months he had reached a point where he could be moved to a new carer, Kerrie (pictured), as he was off medication altogether and was going really well. Rusty has now been adopted into a family that includes a small fluffy dog as his companion. He is now the happiest of dogs and shows no sign of the terrible abuse that he once suffered.

Natalie and Millie

Millie is a bit over two years old. Natalie adopted her shortly before the pair moved to Beechworth, a famous little town in Victoria's north with many historic buildings.

Here, Millie is exploring the old police lock-up where bushranger Ned Kelly was kept in 1871.

Guinness

Guinness originally came from the Mildura pound. He was adopted from AWDRI by the Fox family in Bentleigh, Melbourne, to join their existing dogs Bonnie and Clyde.

His name was chosen for his resemblance to the famous Irish drop. Many people comment on how handsome he is, often mistaking him for a Rottweiler pup. He is an energetic little character who has slotted into city/beach life with ease. His favourite thing is racing back and forwards along the beach chasing seagulls. He also likes going to the park, where he has a gang of fur friends he likes to hang out with.

'I wanted another rescue to
remember my old boy by.'

Heather, Dart and Bentlee

Heather writes: Bentlee (left) is a black and tan kelpie that I
adopted from Victoria after she was rescued from a neglectful
owner. She was flea-ridden and full of worms and was bought
back to health by her foster mum. I adopted Bentlee after I had
lost my old boy (whom I had rescued after he had been shot)
and I wanted another rescue to remember him by.

Bentlee has been in a number of TV commercials around
the world and also competes in agility and flyball. She knows a
number of really cool tricks and is such a loyal, loving dog.

Dart (right) is a red koolie x kelpie that came from the Griffith
Pound. She is currently learning to compete in agility and flyball.
Eventually I would like to do some herding with her as she is
totally switched on and such a natural.

Nimble at Bondi Beach,
Sydney.

Out and About

AWDRI is a nationwide organisation so our work takes us all over the country. And we love to catch up with our former charges wherever they are, from urban Bondi Beach to the outback.

A group of Victorian foster carers and adopters at Brighton Beach.

Nimble and Stevie
with a great Aussie
icon, the Boxing
Kangaroo, painted
on a bathing box
at Brighton Beach,
Melbourne.

Surf's up

Bondi Beach is Sydney's most famous strip of sand. 'Bondi' or 'Boondi' is a Dharug word meaning 'water breaking over rocks' or 'noise of water breaking over rocks'. Bondi Surf Bathers Life Saving Club claims to be the world's first surf lifesaving club.

Classic cars and classic dogs. Black and Tan goes with Blue!

The mighty
Murray River

Jaffa's on a roll!

Dogs by the Tucker Box

The Dog on the Tucker Box monument is located at Snake Gully, eight kilometres from Gundagai, New South Wales. It was unveiled by the then Prime Minister of Australia Joseph Lyons in 1932 as a tribute to local pioneers. The statue was inspired by a bullock drover's poem, 'Bullocky Bill', which celebrates the life of a drover's dog that loyally guarded the man's tucker box until death.

Nikki (in photo) owns the two living, breathing dogs in this scene: Jaffa (left) and Ike (right) who is a foster fail. He was surrendered to a pound at around eight years old due to deafness and neurologically caused incontinence. He is extremely affectionate, always smiling, and won Nikki's heart on day one, with adoption confirmed within a fortnight of arrival.

Adelaide icon

Nimble's pictured outside St Peter's Cathedral in Adelaide. The Anglican cathedral, a city landmark, is situated the corner of Pennington Terrace and King William Road in the suburb of North Adelaide.

Cunningham Pier meet-up

Cunningham Pier is the most famous structure on the Geelong waterfront. Opening in the mid 1850s, the pier was a vital part of the Victorian port city, with rail being used to load and unload cargo. The post-war modernisation of Geelong's ports saw many larger ships move to Corio Quay, and Cunningham Pier gradually fell into disuse. The pier is now the location of one of the city's finest restaurants and is a great place for local AWDRI adopters, carers and their furry friends to meet.

Legends of the turf

AWDRI's South Australian dogs are so special they got an invitation to play on the newly revamped Adelaide Oval. Being the special dogs they are, not one of them dug a hole in the freshly laid turf that was being prepared for the first Adelaide game of the 2015 Cricket World Cup. Good dogs!

Aussie Icons

A gathering of true Australian icons. Above: Barrie Robran, South Australian footballing legend. Below: a black and tan kelpie and a blue Australian cattle dog.

The Victorian high country is a beautiful part of the world and a great place to take just about any dog for a walk. This lookout near Beechworth offers a commanding view of Mount Buffalo.

Nimble 'guarding' the
Australian War Memorial,
Canberra.

High flyers

At the home of the Richmond Tigers, Punt Road Oval in Melbourne, Nimble and Ralph pose for star player Ben Griffiths. Although Ben can jump higher than this pair, they are no slouches at the high jump. Ralph has a PB of 2.55 metres while Nimble is not far behind at 2.45 metres.

Desert dog

Desert covers 1,371,000 square kilometres or 18 per cent of the Australian mainland. The Australian working dog breeds are some of the hardiest in the world, capable of working on huge, hot and dusty cattle stations in outback and desert regions.

Acknowledgments

The making of this book comes from the talents, care and compassion of many people. It's not just a collection of pictures, but stories that have been put together in real life, by real people, doing what we consider to be heroic deeds; saving lives!

I would like to thank my fellow photography contributors, being my gorgeous wife Di Edwards, who is the backbone of everything we do, and Haylie Williams of Photography By Heili, who at the time of writing is the current MDBA Photographer of the Year for her work with AWDRI (and who took the photos 'Ruth: Army recruit'. p.101, and 'Suvi and Merle', p153), along with a few who took photographs of pound animals, abuse cases, and veterinary care instances. A few others along the way who always seem to be around to help out in any way they can include Steve Sudero from Yarra Valley Working Dogs, Sharon Pearson from Mt Lofty Ranges Vineyard, Paul Macphail from Beloka Kelpie Stud, and Scott Williams from Jetpets. Your advice and support is always appreciated!

Of course this book would not have been possible without the people who make up the organisation that is Australian Working Dog Rescue, those people being the volunteers, who not only provide the passion and care required to give these second hand dogs a second chance at life, but make that chance more likely to succeed than most would ever think possible. These people are the life blood of what we do in every area the organisation works in. It would be near impossible to even consider naming them all, so I hope that every single one of them knows how much they are appreciated and admired!

Thanks must also go to ABC Books for pushing this project of mine forward, and in particular to Katie Stackhouse, who has kept pushing me along while the rest of life has been so busy I have sometimes neglected to keep up with the project. Rescue can be distracting and all consuming!

Lastly, I want to thank the dogs. Not just my own dogs, but all the AWDRI dogs out there. I wish I could get to meet you all as I used to when we first started this journey of rescue. The joy, enthusiasm and trust that you exhibit towards life, and we humans, is something I can only admire, and I, along with all of my colleagues, will continue to strive to do what we think is the best we can do for you all.

Carey Edwards.
Forever AWDRI.

 The ABC 'Wave' device is a trademark of the
Australian Broadcasting Corporation and is used
under licence by HarperCollins*Publishers* Australia

 All royalties from the sale of this book, and any proceeds
from direct sales by Australian Working Dog Rescue (AWDRI),
go to AWDRI.

First published in Australia in 2015
by HarperCollins*Publishers* Australia Pty Limited
ABN 36 009 913 517
harpercollins.com.au

HarperCollinsPublishers
Level 13, 201 Elizabeth Street, Sydney NSW 2000, Australia
Unit D1, 63 Apollo Drive, Rosedale, Auckland 0632, New Zealand
A 53, Sector 57, Noida, UP, India
1 London Bridge Street, London, SE1 9GF, United Kingdom
2 Bloor Street East, 20th floor, Toronto, Ontario M4W 1A8, Canada
195 Broadway, New York NY 10007, USA

ISBN 978 0 7333 3454 2

Cover photography by Carey Edwards/AWDRI (front) and Haylie Williams/Photography By Heili (back)
Cover design by Hazel Lam, HarperCollins Design Studio
Internal design by Sam Williams
Typeset in Whitney by Tobias Frere-Jones
Colour reproduction by Graphic Print Group, Adelaide, South Australia
Printed and bound in China by RR Donnelley

6 5 4 3 2   16 17 18 19